14 February 05

To my Darling

The Poet's Child

Making a decision
to have a child is
momentous. It is to
decide forever to have
your heart go walking
around outside your
body.

E. STONE

The Poet's Child

EDITED BY MICHAEL WIEGERS

COPPER CANYON PRESS

Cover art: Untitled (boy as bird), by Ralph Eugene Meatyard (1925–1972), 1960/print 1981 by Christopher Meatyard. Gelatin silver print, 15.1 x 15.2 cm. Thanks to Christopher and Diane Meatyard and the George Eastman House for making it possible to use this photograph on the cover.

Copper Canyon Press would like to thank Art Hanlon for his assistance with this book, as well as for supplying its title.

Copper Canyon Press is in residence under the auspices of the Centrum Foundation at Fort Worden State Park in Port Townsend, Washington. Centrum sponsors artist residencies, education workshops for Washington State students and teachers, Blues, Jazz, and Fiddletunes Festivals, classical music performances, and The Port Townsend Writers' Conference.

Library of Congress Cataloging-in-Publication Data
The poet's child / edited by Michael Wiegers.
    p. cm.
ISBN 1-55659-175-6 (alk. paper)
1. Children—Poetry. 2. Parent and child—Poetry. I. Wiegers, Michael.
PN6110.C4 P56 2002
808.81'9352054—dc21

                    2002006262

9 8 7 6 5 4 3 2 first printing

COPPER CANYON PRESS
Post Office Box 271
Port Townsend, Washington 98368
www.coppercanyonpress.org

Contents

FOR KATE AND ELLA

ALL HERE

for Ella Addison Wiegers, b. xi:99

Body of dew, mind
of empty sky—the prelude
and the afterword

*

Under bare willows,
pond frogs sing about old age
while girls dream of princes

Obaka the Pilgrim

Introduction

As a parent—and let me say right from the start that I came to parenting reluctantly—I often find myself in the position of trying to describe things to my daughter, Ella. Part of this process of explaining leads us to stories and poems and songs. We often make things up as we go along. As she has grown older, she has moved beyond parroting her parents' words, her participation in these stories becoming greater. These ongoing poems and stories become part of our family life.

This was true even in our first days together as father and daughter. At night as we went to sleep, or during the day out on walks, I'd read aloud or try to conjure poems and songs, partly for her sake, partly for my own. The poems weren't always easy. I kept fighting off memories of the truths of the Sylvia Plath poems I'd read as a teenager, or of Philip Larkin's famous "This Be The Verse," which ends:

> Man hands on misery to man.
> It deepens like a coastal shelf.
> Get out as early as you can,
> And don't have any kids yourself.

I'd usually try to find some other, replacement words to echo the complexity of my new emotions in those nervous first days of parenthood. The nervousness and doubt have lessened a bit as the range of expression has grown. While our relationship develops, I find that the common warnings that would-be parents hear (e.g., "It's hard work! There's no time for art . . ."), are just as unsatisfactory as common, sentimental celebrations (e.g., "It's the greatest thing you'll ever do . . ."). It's not that these sentiments aren't valid; they are simply insufficient. In fact, they become annoying, whether you're a parent or not.

I've cast my lot with poetry as a profession, and poetry seems as well the most appropriate manner of capturing, and celebrating, the complex and paradoxical emotions of the family dynamic. Poetry can elucidate complexity—particularly emotional complexity—more than the prose of how-to books, and the poems that I remembered and later searched for taught me that my nervousness about becoming a parent was in fact pretty normal. So were my fears, doubts, and particularly those altogether strange new joys. We are complicated, not-always-loving beings, as many poets have written when faced with the role of parenting. Conversely, simple things about our family, so simple that they evade words, are cause for great enjoyment. Yet poets have demonstrated that we don't need to satisfy ourselves by casually stating that the experience is "indescribable." Paraphrase will not do. Maybe poems will.

In *The Gift of Tongues,* Copper Canyon's founding editor Sam Hamill explains how poetry exists in a "gift economy":

> the gift of inspiration is transformed by the
> poet into a body of sound which in turn is
> given away so that it may inspire and inform
> another, who in turn adds to the gift and
> gives it away again.

The poet's gift is a risky one, particularly when it engages sentiment; it's not given in the hope of some sort of return, and more often is met with either silence or criticism rather than praise or gratitude. It's an economy similar to the "family" economy, in which we give to one another in what similarly seem to be ordinary ways. One of the gifts that emboldened me as a parent was a poem by Gregory Orr, which ends: "I try to teach her caution; / she tries to teach me risk." Ella has brought risk back into my "intense uninteresting life," as Thomas McGrath has written. Once, I could not have imagined life as a parent, just as once I never could have imagined a life immersed in poetry. Now, I cannot imagine life otherwise. I risk sentimentality and cliché in saying so.

Bringing children into the world, an act that one could argue is selfish, even foolish, invites trouble. It invites risk. Again, so does poetry. But then it was Ella who taught me to recognize why poets have risked so much by writing about children, about families. On one of our daily walks, before she had experienced her first spring, we were taking a shortcut off the neighborhood streets and through a local farmer's fields where there were sheep and horses, a llama even (all to figure into future stories and adventures). We would stop to talk with the animals before pressing on to the edge of the fields, where a small opening through some bushes and brambles gave way to a path through a forest of cedars, firs, wild rhododendrons. I had been running a poem over and over in my memory, as something eventually to give to her, and was lost in the moment of the poem. At the same time that I was lost in my thoughts, my daughter was just discovering her world. I was distant from the immediate moment of my daughter, there on the edge of the field. We came to the forest entrance where overnight the Scotch broom on either side had broken into brilliant yellow bloom. Here was a child's first flower, a beautiful ditch weed that I casually discarded but which stunned her new eyes. We paused as she reached out, then examined the plant closely, its every detail coming into focus.

She would later have similar experiences with crows flying over a cloud-covered ridge in the Olympic Mountains, or with rocks on the beach as a winter gale was blowing up, and she continues to do so now, as she grows older and collects the sounds of new words and plays with the various ways of putting them together. Each time, she teaches me that I am missing the smallest details, hidden surprises, and elemental moments and sounds I so much love in my favorite poems. She is teaching me the intrinsic lesson of poetry: poetry allows us to recover a little bit of our world, and through it we open up to yet one more perspective. In the best poems, we are forced to experience the world anew, through fresh eyes. I'd further risk sentimentality by arguing that a poem can even give us back some innocence as it gives us knowledge. It can help us rediscover the world and its languages—including the world and languages of our own complicated children and families.

Michael Wiegers

The Poet's Child

YOU TAUGHT ME

All those years, alone,
Married to the intense uninteresting life . . .
And, until you came, Tomasito,
I didn't even know my name!

Thomas McGrath

The Hand:
"Brightness Falls from the Air"
for my daughter at three months

Maybe you thought it was a bird
or some other strange and harmless
creature fluttering in attendance
as you lay on your back in the crib.

But today I watched as you held
your hand inches above your face,
gazed a long, unknowing moment
then suddenly understood its splayed
star-shape was yourself.

                You screamed.
I lifted you up and held you close
and all the while I felt you
falling toward our world.

Gregory Orr

AGAINST WRITING ABOUT CHILDREN

When I think of the many people
who privately despise children,
I can't say I'm completely shocked,

having been one. I was not
exceptional, uncomfortable as that is
to admit, and most children are not

exceptional. The particulars of
cruelty, sizes Large and X-Large,
memory gnawing it like

a fat dog, are ordinary: Mean Miss
Smigelsky from the sixth grade;
the orthodontist who

slapped you for crying out. Children
frighten us, other people's and
our own. They reflect

the virused figures in which failure
began. We feel accosted by their
vulnerable natures. Each child turns

into a problematic ocean, a mirrored
body growing denser and more
difficult to navigate until

sunlight merely bounces
off the surface. They become impossible
to sound. Like us, but even weaker.

Erin Belieu

THE DOLL BELIEVERS

This lifeless construction,
Yellow hair curled and twisted,
The forever motionless face of rubber,
The dark marked eyebrows,
The flexible pug nose,
Spongy red cheeks,
Camel's-hair eyebrows
Moving up and down.
Lifting her up, her eyes fly open,
They stare into space—
An unmoving blueness.
Those never winking, moving balls,
Controlled from the inside,
And that thick rubber body,
The imprint of a navel,
The undersized hands,
The thick soft knees,
The screwed-on head,
The air hole behind her neck,
All this in its lifelessness
Gives me a feeling
That children are amazing
To imagine such a thing alive.

Clarence Major

MUSE

In later years, my daughter said to me
that when she was little and before
sister and brother, growing up in that trailer
that bordered the desert, she thought there was someone
else who lived with us, and it was only later that she knew
there was no one else, just the poetry, that other child that I was
                                                    always singing to,
nursing in my arms, chanting, as I passed back and forth between
                                                    those rooms.

Rebecca Seiferle

WHAT EFFECT HAS YOUR NEW SON HAD ON YOUR WRITING LIFE?

While Andrew sleeps
in the room that used to be my study
I go downstairs to a desk
in a corner of the basement
to write. And each day when he wakes
I sit him in my lap and keep working,
bouncing him on my knee and typing
like I used to, quickly with one finger,
reciting lines to see
if my poems put him to sleep.
That's heaven—writing poetry,
Andrew in my arms. Though I abandon
the most divinely inspired poem when
Andrew wants his bottle.

Richard Jones

AFTER KUO CHU-PU'S POEMS

(an excerpt)

Trees thick and full gathering pure
midsummer shade out front, and wind

coming in its season, gentle gusts
opening my robe—I live life apart

here. Cultivating idleness, I roam
koto strings and books all day long,

our vegetable garden full of plenty,
last year's grain holding out well.

In making a living, we gain by limits.
Wanting nothing beyond enough, nothing,

I grind millet, make up a lovely wine,
and when it's ripe, ladle it out myself.

Our son plays beside me. Too young
to speak, he keeps trying new sounds.

All this brings back such joy I forget
glittering careers. White clouds drift

endless skies. I watch. Why all that
reverent longing for ancient times?

T'ao Ch'ien
translated from the Chinese
by David Hinton

The Murmur

The doctor flicks on a light,
puts up the X rays of our three-day-old child,
and diagnoses a shunt between
left and right ventricle,
claims an erratic electrocardiogram test
confirms his findings. Your child,
he says, may live three to six weeks unless
surgery is performed.

Two days later, a pediatric cardiologist
looks at the same X rays and EKG test,
pronounces them normal,
and listens with disinterest to the murmur.
I think, then, of the birth:
mother and child in a caesarean,
the rush of blood in the umbilical cord
is a river pulsating with light.

And, as water rippling in a pond
ricochets off rocks, the network of
feelings between father and mother
and child is an ever-shifting web.
It is nothing on your doctor's X ray
scanner; but, like minerals lit up
under a black light, it is an iridescent
red and green and indigo.

Arthur Sze

THREE BODIES

A pregnant woman
lies at night by her man.
In her belly
a child moved.
"Put your hand on my belly,"
says the woman.
"What moved so lightly
is a tiny hand or leg
of our child.
It will be mine and yours
though only I have to bear it."

The man nestles close to her,
they both feel the same.
In the woman a child moves.

And the three bodies pool their warmth
at night, when a pregnant woman
lies by her man.

Anna Swir
translated from the Polish
by Czesław Miłosz and Leonard Nathan

A NATURALIST

. . . to his unborn daughter

I've waited a long time,
little one, longer than a man
is supposed to, wandering
the diminished coast,
searching for extinct whales,
the migrating iris—
some small, unclaimed breath
among the waves.

Will you come to feel
that all of this is for us,
that bringing you
into our imagined world
was a selfish act?
I wonder, snarl at my reflection
and shudder, then smile
like a pickerel,
hoping against hope.

Be patient, my love.
Don't kick too hard
or drink your rage.
You are the long blue dawn
of every dying life.
And we can only ask.

William O'Daly

KING'S DAUGHTERS, HOME FOR
UNWED MOTHERS, 1948

Somewhere there figures a man. In uniform. He's not white. He
could be AWOL. Sitting on a mattress riddled with cigarette burns.
Night of a big game in the capital. Big snow.
Beyond Pearl River past Petal and Leaf River and Macedonia;
it is a three-storied house. The only hill around. White.
The house and hill are white. Lighted upstairs, down.
She is up on her elbows, bangs wet in her eyes. The head
of the unborn is visible at the opening. The head
crowns. Many helping hands are on her. She is told not to push.
But breathe. A firm voice. With helping hands.
They open the howl of her love. Out of her issues:

Volumes of letters, morning glories on a string trellis, the job at the
Maybelline factory, the job at the weapons plant, the hummingbird
hive, her hollyhocks, her grandmother's rigid back next to her
grandfather's bow, the briefest reflection of her mother's braid,
her atomizers and silver-backed brush and comb, the steel balls
under her father's knuckles, the moon's punched-out face,
his two-dollar neckties, the peacock coming down the drive; there was
the boy shuffling her way with the melon on his shoulder, car dust all
over his light clothes, the Black Cat fireworks sign on the barn, her
father's death from moving the barn by himself, the family
    sitting in the
darkened room drinking ice tea after the funeral, tires blown
    out on the
macadam, the women beaten like eggs, the store with foundation
garments, and boys pelting the girls with peony buds, the meatgrinder
cringing in the corner store, the old icebox she couldn't fix and

couldn't sell so buried to keep out the kids, her grandmother's
    pride, the
prettiest lavaliere, the pole houses; there was the boy with the melon
shifted to the other shoulder, coming her way, grown taller and darker,
wiping his sweat with his hand, his beautiful Nubian head,
    older and set
upon by the longingly necked girls from the bottoms, his fishing hole,
learning the equations of equality: six for the white man and none for
the rest; the sloping shadows and blue hollows behind his shack, what
the sunflowers saw, the wide skirts she wore, the lizards
    they caught, the
eagerness with which they went through each other's folds of hair and
skin, the boy's outnumbered pride ...

This couldn't go on, the difficulty of concealment, putting makeup
over a passion mark. 1947, summer of whiskey and victory and
fear. It was long, then over. The letters burned. She heaves. Bleeds.
The infant's head is huge. She tears. He's white. He'll make it
just fine. The firm voice. The hands that helped.
What would become of this boychild. The uniformed man and she
will never know. That they will outlive him. They will never know.
Whether he will do things they never dreamed.

C.D. Wright

JUNE 20

i will be born in one week
to a frowned forehead of a woman
and a man whose fingers will itch
to enter me. she will crochet
a dress for me of silver
and he will carry me in it.
they will do for each other
all that they can
but it will not be enough.
none of us know that we will not
smile again for years,
that she will not live long.
in one week i will emerge face first
into their temporary joy.

Lucille Clifton

". . . AS SOFT AND AS PINK AS A NURSERY . . ."

This is the good child
in his bed. Beside him, his mother
with her sweet pink face, her nice
manners, her extremely well-manicured
fingers, her strange desire to have him
perfectly untouched, so that her hands
are always running over him,
pushing his hair back and exposing
his hot, gleaming face, wiping
his nose with the edge
of her tissue, picking
at things on his clothes: little bits
of thread, dust, food, lint
of a world that clings to him
almost lovingly—these she assiduously removes
as if she were his valet
grooming him for a starring role, the curtain
about to go up, and only her between him
and the humiliating abyss
of some unforgivable gaffe,
the laughter of strangers . . .

this is the good mother
who, as the light fades to mauve
and the corners begin to fill with distended
shadows, reads him stories full of vengeful,
hairy, bad-tempered and evil-smelling
monsters, huge as Hindenburgs, engorged
with centuries of crimes imagined

in millions of nurseries, waxing
in the growing dark of bedtime; genies
festering with long imprisonment—planning
at first, gold and deep gratitude
to their rescuers; later, after years
in the jar, beginning to plot
the gifts that bring ruin; finally,
bloated with a rage
so murderous, so purely tabloid
and horribly true, that to lift out the cork
were to loose Pandora's swarm of evils
without a hope to flutter after . . .

the little boy can do nothing but watch
as these colossal figures fill the little space
that is his room, their thick legs rising
like the trunks of redwoods, their distant
shoulders looming like cliffs, their necks
periscopes peering into the black intangible
sky, from where he hears, booming,
the arrogant thunder of their laughter
so that even the stars are shaken
as if the night were a thick black mass
of icy gelatin in which the stars
were caught, shivering and burning . . .

he draws himself up tight under the quilt,
a still, small mound that watches
round-eyed as the monsters pour
from the pink heart-shaped mouth
of his mother, who now and then smiles sweetly,
calls him her little man, her bug, her pet,
and fiddles with the button at her neck.

Eleanor Wilner

Childish

Take your kids away, take them,
you who teach them to yell "hooray!" when excited.
It's profoundly untrue.
(Likewise, close the crematory oven,
what if the sideburns of a distracted onlooker catch fire
at the observation window, which is still scalding after
    incinerating Mom.)
Our representatives travel to streets, racetracks, bakeries
—easily recognized by the nursing bottles embroidered on their
    blue caps—
and to those kids who whine beyond description,
they hand out candy, toys, tricycles, atomic bombs
that can generate radioactive mushrooms at least five feet tall.
What we mustn't permit, however, is spitting,
which is truly unbearable.
In these days devoted to the science of child-rearing I climb up to
    the roof over and over again,
to take walks and unwind:
across the maritime horizon I see
giant distant whales go by.

Gerardo Deniz
translated from the Spanish
by Mónica de la Torre

MATERNITY

I gave birth to life.
It went out of my entrails
and asks for the sacrifice of my life
as does an Aztec deity.
I lean over a little puppet,
we look at each other
with four eyes.

"You are not going to defeat me," I say.
"I won't be an egg which you would crack
in a hurry for the world,
a footbridge that you would take on the way to your life.
I will defend myself."

I lean over a little puppet,
I notice
a tiny movement of a tiny finger
which a little while ago was still in me,
in which, under a thin skin,
my own blood flows.
And suddenly I am flooded
by a high, luminous wave
of humility.
Powerless, I drown.

Anna Swir
translated from the Polish
by Czesław Miłosz and Leonard Nathan

What Parents Do Not Yet Know

The tree that lingers at the window is just sixteen,
And you, uneasy parent of its wanton ways,
Eavesdrop upon the whispering of three-fingered leaves.

The pale pink squirrel who dances in the nude,
Chattering of nuts, with eyes that see five ways,
Is not related to the tree's anomalies, nor grieves

That you, tormented guardian of bark and roots
And leaves, must seek for words to ratify the pact.
You were once witness to departing wings that fled defiantly

One winter night; hear now the fragile music as it weaves
Like ivy through the cawing of the crows. Not wasp, or cattle ant,
    or bee
Is hesitant, for each believes his paragon of industry is what
Transforms a tree to a child, and child to tree again
        (with softly whispering leaves.)

Kay Boyle

What We Need Words For

Each morning, his baby fingers clack
on the electronic keys of the obsolete typewriter
that my father left us when he died,
and what my son hears and loves is the sound
of his own fingers clattering into the world, the zing
of the carriage return, the space bar like a runaway train
clicking through the letters that he is only beginning
to recognize, the hunt and peck
of his own name.

We all stumble into ourselves
like this, fitting our fingers to the shape of letters,
while the page gallops out of our reach,
and, though he's only five, it's loss that drives him
to the words, trying to pick out his own name
among whatever is attached to himself, whatever
he longs to answer, relating each day
a letter to his sister, now gone from home,
far away in college.

The page, when it rolls off the cylinder,
is full of the rhythm of his furious
digits, all drive and urgency of expression,
a jumble of letters and numbers, not words,
not legible text, but a sea of drift,
and, yet, at times, in the broken lines,

a name, a word, floats up into view—
the first legibility of the heart, its exacting
infancy— *lluv luve yur broder Jacob*.

Rebecca Seiferle

THE THERMOS

Poppy seeds from a North Bennington garden
rest in white envelopes on a *granero*
in Jacona—*to travel far is to return.*
I am not thinking about the glitter of snow

on top of Popocatepetl, but how beauty
that is not beauty requires distance.
I recall the green glow of glacier ice,
bald eagles perched at the tip of Homer Spit.

When I brought home that turtle-shaped
sandbox, we placed a giraffe, lion, tiger
at the edge. Sarah was happy to pour sand
from her yellow shovel into a blue pail.

I poured sand into a funnel and watched it
drain into the box. I do not know how
an amethyst crystal begins to take shape;
I do not know the nanoproperties of

silica or the origin of light, but I
know the moment a seed bursts its husk.
At work I pour tea out of a thermos,
smell your hair and how we quicken each other.

Arthur Sze

WHAT NO ONE COULD HAVE TOLD THEM

Once he comes to live on the outside of her, he will not sleep
through the night or the next 400. He sleeps not, they sleep not.
Ergo they steer gradually mad. The dog's head shifts another
paw under the desk. Over a period of 400 nights.

You will see, she warns him. Life is full of television sets,
invoices, organs of other animals thawing on counters.

In her first dream of him, she leaves him sleeping on Mamo's
salt-bag quilt behind her alma mater. Leaves him to the Golden
Goblins. Sleep, pretty one, sleep.

*. . . the quilt that comforted her brother's youthful bed, the
quilt he took to band camp.*

Huh oh, he says, Huh oh. His word for many months.
Merrily pouring a bottle of Pledge over the dog's dull coat. And
with a round little belly that shakes like jelly.

Waiting out a shower in the Border Cafe; the bartender
spoons a frozen strawberry into his palm-leaf basket while they
lift their frosted mugs in a grateful click.

He sits up tall in his grandfather's lap, waving and waving to
the Blue Bonnet truck. Bye, blue, bye.

In the next dream he stands on his toes, executes a flawless
flip onto the braided rug. Resprings to crib.

The salt-bag quilt goes everywhere, the one the bitch
Rosemary bore her litters on. The one they wrap around the
mower, and bundle with black oak leaves.

How the bowl of Quick Quaker Oats fits his head.

He will have her milk at 1:42, 3:26, 4 a.m. Again at 6. Bent
over the rail to settle his battling limbs down for an afternoon
nap. Eyes shut, trying to picture what in the world she has on.

His nightlight—a snow-white pair of porcelain owls.

They remember him toothless, with one tooth, two tooths,
five or seven scattered around in his head. They can see the day
when he throws open his jaw to display several vicious rows.

Naked in a splash of sun, he pees into a paper plate the guest
set down in the grass as she reached for potato chips.

Suppertime, the dog takes leave of the desk's cool cavity to
patrol his highchair.

How patiently he pulls Kleenex from a box. Tissue by tissue.
How quietly he stands at the door trailing the White Cloud;
swabs his young hair with the toilet brush.

The dog inherits the salt-bag quilt. The one her Mamo made
when she was seventeen—girlfriends stationed around a frame in black stockings
sewing, talking about things their children would do;

He says: cereal, byebye, shoe, raisin, nobody. He hums.

She stands before the medicine chest, drawn. Swiftly he tumps discarded Tampax and hair from an old comb into her tub.

Wearily the man enters the house through the back. She isn't dressed. At the table there is weeping. Curses. Forking dried breasts of chicken.

while Little Sneed sat on the floor beneath the frame, pushing the needles back through.

One yawn followed by another yawn. Then little fists screwing little eyes. The wooden crib stuffed with bears and windup pillows wheeled in to receive him. Out in a twinkle. The powdered bottom airing the dark. The 400th night. When they give up their last honeyed morsel of love; the dog nestles in the batting of the salt-bag quilt commencing its long mope unto death.

C.D. Wright

DAUGHTER

I look
carefully around the
door to see
your face sweet
like a child in a dream
you sleep.
What are
you
dreaming
in your child's mind?
You spent the last hour
of your day
in misery,
toes and knees that hurt,
dolls falling over,
bottles empty;
tears invaded your
cheeks while
over and over
you tossed the blankets off
pleading, *Cover me.*
What's making you cry?
I wanted to know
and held you
as you climbed away
as I sighed,
I'm tired,
let me rest,
go to sleep, my daughter.

Susan Griffin

The Last Thing I Say

to a thirteen-year-old sleeping,
tone of an angel, breath of a soft wing,
I say through an upright dark space
as I narrow it pulling the door
sleepily to let the words go surely into
the bedroom until I close them in
for good, a night watchman's—worth
of grace and a promise for morning
not so far from some God's first notion
that the world be an image by first light
so much better than pictures of hope
drawn by firelight in ashes,
so much clearer, too, a young person
wanting to be a man might draw one finger
along an edge of this world and it
would slice a mouth there
to speak blood and then should he put that wound
into the mouth of his face,
he will be kissed there and taste
the salt of his father as he lowers
himself from his son's high bedroom
in the heaven of his image of
a small part of himself and sweet dreams.

Marvin Bell

READING A STORY TO MY CHILD

This is a small boy
In a ragged coat.
Moving through his world
Is a bold paintbrush
Briefing on the light in the dark.

In the most subtle way
You are drawn to the heart
Because the heart is the name
Of the story,
But you do not know this yet.

He is going to school:
Though you know he must first
Cross the lake,
Whistle to the birds,
And clean out an understanding path
In the tall grass.

He is a good boy
Who adores crows;
He even talks like them.

He is no fool;
He will not hurt you.
He does not talk;
He lives an honest life.

At school, the children
Abhor him.

They see clothes
And the disaster of no voice.
What kind of school is this
That abhors true love?

He may not eat much,
But they are starved.
Boy, you are in the tall grass
And the soil is ruthless.

What do they teach here
That is as nice as our eyes closed?
The school is on a strange page
Farther away than the lines of the smallest trees.
And each parted brushstroke
Is like a squadron of geese.

But the little boy
Holds on to his heart.
(*Yes Sir*) It is better than a bright nickel,
Or a ball,
Or a tall pole.

He does not know
Quite how to write.
He thinks language
Is a series of bizarre pictures.

Though it is loud
It is not sharp like a crow's voice CAW CAW CAW.
And it is not bright
Like a birthday of new flowers.

(*Yes Sir*)
In all of the fields that he knows,
These pictures are not wise—
And he knows this.

At a certain point, there is more
Color on the page
Than in the eyes of a dove
That is listening.

He looks out of the window—
Home.
Someone there who knows him—
Softly and hard
Sees our storm;
Its ruthlessness
And its subtle tentacles of rain
We have all absorbed.

Hey,
But this is a boy who holds on.
My, you'd want to know this boy.
Now I am on page 8
And afraid for my soul.
At this point I say,
Boy.
(*Yes Sir*)
I say, Boy
Hold on for us all.

But today, he is given a brush.
He has climbed all the way down

And he has climbed back up
On his strange way that gets here,
And because he is not afraid
Darkness does not hide him.
He knows its crows
And their love is prehistoric

Like shale at the gorge,
Like evening cold,
Like the lonely gills of a fat fish
At the edge of water.

My, my, my,
You'd love this boy
Just for how it feels.

He paints birds at that
Exact moment flight enflames us.
He sees their heads as small prayers
On the lips of the sky.

(*Yes Sir*)
He knows how—this boy;
He knows how their wings are
Soft, ironic smiles that are alive.

My, my, my,
How Daddy cries. (*Yes Sir*)
This here is just a boy he knows
And won't say why.
A small boy
In a ragged coat.

Primus St. John

A Daughter's Fever

Dark ivy draws a wave across the yard,
even the shadows
are streaked with rain. Light drizzles the oak leaves
and I rock behind this screen,
listening to squirrels, the bickering of jays.
The five a.m. garbage truck
doesn't wake you
as it scrapes the curb from can to can.
Three hours of crying lit the windows next door,
but now you lie as quiet
as the rain. After the dozen books,
the trail we frayed from piano
to puppets, to the cardboard frog
on his pond of cut wool,
I lean to your blanket
and hold my breath.

Rachel, about the little girl
who started home late
across the darkening woods . . .
Someday I'll give you the words I used all night
to guide her home. So many ways
to enter the forest and never return.
But happily that's another ending.

Under a basket of cornflowers
hung from the mantel,
she sleeps now in her cottage near the town.
Her father watches

new light clothe the trees.
In his orchard
the crows out-cackle the squirrels.
He holds his breath to hear
her breathe, around his finger
small fingers curl.

David Bottoms

PITTSBURGH

And my beautiful daughter
had her liver cut open in Pittsburgh.
My god, my god! I rubbed
her back over the swollen and wounded
essentiality, I massaged
her legs, and we talked of death.
At the luckiest patients with liver cancer have
a 20% chance. We might have talked
of my death, not long to come. But no,
the falling into death of a beautiful
young woman is so much more important.
A wonderful hospital. If I must die
away from my cat Smudge and my Vermont Castings stove
let it be at Allegheny General.
I read to her, a novella by Allan Gurganus,
a Russian serious flimsiness by Voinovich,
and we talked. We laughed. We actually
laughed. I bought her a lipstick
which she wore though she disliked the color.
Helicopters took off and landed on the hospital pad,
bringing hearts and kidneys and maybe livers
from other places to be transplanted
into people in the shining household of technology
by shining technologists, wise and kindly.
The chances are so slight. Oh, my daughter,
my love for you has burgeoned—
an excess of singularity ever increasing—
you are my soul—for forty years. You

still beautiful and young. In my hotel
I could not sleep. In my woods, on my
little farm, in the blizzard on the mountain,
I could not sleep either, but scribbled
fast verses, very fast and
wet with my heartsblood and brainjuice
all my life, as now
in Pittsburgh. I don't know which of
us will live the longer, it's all a flick
of the wrist of the god mankind invented
and then had to deinvent, such a failure, like all
our failures, and the worst and best
is sentimentality after all. Let us go out together.
Here in brutal Pittsburgh. Let us
be together in the same room,
the old poet and the young painter,
holding hands, a calm touch, a whisper,
as the thumping helicopters go out and come in,
we in the crisis of forever inadequately medicated
pain, in the love of daughter and father.

Hayden Carruth

Magic Words to Cure a Sick Child

O my tiny child
my breasts are dripping with milk
for you
open your mouth and suck
drink
climb the mountain
up at the top you'll be healthy
you'll live a long long time

an Inuit song
adaptation by Stephen Berg

The Windows

Here is a child who presses his head to the ground
his eyes are open
he sees through one window
the flat gray ocean
upside down
with an arbor of islands hanging from it
all the way to the horizon
and he himself is hanging from nothing
he might step down
and walk on the old sky far down there
out to the clouds
in the far islands
he might step on the clouds where they have worn shiny
he might jump from cloud to cloud
he watches lights flash
on and off along the dark shores
and the lights moving among the overhead islands
he feels his head like a boat on a beach
he hears the waves break around his ears
he stands up and listens
he turns to a room full of his elders
and the lights on
blue day in the far empty windows
and without moving he flies

W.S. Merwin

THREE PIECES OF CANDY

I'm dizzy from hunger
and the child is pale as paper—
says mother to father
when we walk in the street.

—So buy each of us a bonbon
—says father.
—I have no money—
says mother.

And she buys each of us
a bonbon.
—Anyway, it gives you strength—
says mother.

We smile,
all three of us.
We taste. Three paradises melt
in our mouths.

Anna Swir
translated from the Polish
by Czesław Miłosz and Leonard Nathan

DON'T FORGET

I was always called in early for dinner.
It was dusk usually, half an inning to go,
I'd hear my mother tell me to beat the dark,
everyone would mumble, I'd throw my glove down and leave.

At home, sitting at the table, I'd imagine the score,
and the speckled homework book seemed to watch me
until I opened it, stared at the numbers, and fell asleep.
Damp laundry rustled in the yards of the houses.

Everyone was punished like this because
our parents worried we'd fall, or missed us,
but we always got hurt anyway or would sit for hours
sanding the wings of an enemy fighter plane until they shined

like metal. We climbed walls until we slipped and our legs broke,
our first kisses were so murderous we almost fainted.
Don't forget, this is inside us every day.
We want everything, our hands stop too soon,

and who are we when a face speaks and opens to us
like a wave? The tame grasses of the head, the moist spiral ear,
long water nobody has crossed—you feel yourself leaving,
you can't lift your hands, you stand there, leaving.

Stephen Berg

FATHER'S SONG

Yesterday, against admonishment,
my daughter balanced on the couch back,
fell and cut her mouth.

Because I saw it happen I knew
she was not hurt, and yet
a child's blood's so red
it stops a father's heart.

My daughter cried her tears;
I held some ice
against her lip.
That was the end of it.

Round and round; bow and kiss.
I try to teach her caution;
she tries to teach me risk.

Gregory Orr

Mother to Son

Look, child, I should have mentioned this before.
You're nearly four years old. I didn't think—
or should have realized you were noticing
all your years of watching. So now, Look,
my son, and see how beautiful we are!
In Central Park today the sun's unlocked
the gates of joy, and let loose on the lawn
the people. There's a sound of hop and horn.
And every sprinkler has its worshipers.
Walking here through Harlem, how you laughed

when those three girls hosed our fleeing feet,
calling, "You go, girl," "That boy's a peach."
The corners seemed to smoke with pressed-up heat.
Perhaps I should have named our differences.
The woman's matted hair that's strong as a rope,
beside the jangling man with dazzling teeth,
that ample turbaned gentleman, tent-kneed,
Or there—the blonde who got up, turtle broad.
You're watching how she walks: a turtle stroll.
Street vendors hawk their chilly for a dollar,

by storefront mosques, past Orthodoxim stoles.
Playing with Big John and Ken at school,
you'd make a perfect spectrum, light to dark.
From Nordic white to sleek mahogany,
my Mediterranean Jew, you are the middle
figure in those colors' tritone scale.

So tell me, little man, what should I say
to you who stopped that giant eight-year-old
cold as he was climbing up the fort,
when you shouted down at him,

"No colored boys allowed"?

Jenny Factor

LYNCHING AND BURNING

Men lean toward the wood.
Hoods   crease
Until they find people
Where there used to be hoods.
Instead of a story,
The whole thing becomes a scream
        then time, place, far,
        late in the country,
        alone,
        an old man's farm.
Children we used to call charcoal,
Now they smell that way—deliberately,
And the moon stares at smoke like iced tea.
Daughter,
        Once there was a place we called the earth.
        People lived there. Now we live there . . .

Primus St. John

CHILDHOOD

For each a golden age. The trees brimming
with leaves, the garden's mysterious flowers—
sweet-scented nicotiana, nasturtiums in a pool of sunlight,
mint under the faucet drip—an enclosure
where English walnuts sent long, pollen-dropping blooms
over the driveway. Freesias marched across the lawn
through crimson bells. Sweet peas
climbed by the window.

Hard times, and the gleaners
followed the walnut harvest, or in spring
picked mustard from the fields. Wanderers—hungry men—
came to the back door.

The orchard flung down more than we wanted—
first plums, then peaches, oranges, persimmons,
and the garden shot up scalloped squash
green beans, tomatoes, a profusion.

Sundays we sat among uncles and aunts,
lingered round the oak table, heavy with bounty,
in the far-off age, golden, encircled,
the world falling apart, armies beginning to move.

Ann Stanford

THE AMERICAN CENTURY

Blackbirds whistle over the young
Willow leaves, pale celadon green,
In the cleft of the emerald hills.
My daughter is twenty-one months old.
Already she knows the names of
Many birds and flowers and all
The animals of barnyard and zoo.
She paddles in the stream, chasing
Tiny bright green frogs. She wants
To catch them and kiss them. Now she
Runs to me with a tuft of rose
Gray owl's clover. "What's that? Oh! What's that?"
She hoots like an owl and caresses
The flower when I tell her its name.
Overhead in the deep sky
Of May Day jet bombers cut long
White slashes of smoke. The blackbird
Sings and the baby laughs, midway
In the century of horror.

Kenneth Rexroth

Unnoticed

You drift from youth into manhood
as unnoticed as if you were drifting off to sleep.
You have a past, you sit around facing bottles of hard liquor,
and more and more of your friends become fathers.

Now, the father comes to see you with his little son,
and pretty soon the boy understands you better,
he understands the burning adventures of your heart,
and playing on the floor, together you outwit the seesaw of time.

But the day comes when you make money like a grownup,
you translate on commission, sell poems,
argue about contracts, calculate, protest,
and you too can only make a living with the help of "extras."

You don't look for success, you know it doesn't help.
That lady favors only those who exist at the right time—
You like the poppy and the red-skinned sour cherry
instead of the honey and walnut which fascinate sad teenagers.

And you know that in summer too a leaf can fall,
no matter how much the brain burns and dances,
and that everything will be measured when you're dead.
You can't be a great athlete or a roaming sailor,

but you have learned that the pen is a weapon and a tool
and you can break your neck trying to write an honest poem
and you know this way too you can reach all those places
where intentions are bare and the fires of adventure burn.

And as you write, pressing your weight on the pen, you think
about children, and there is no pride in your sad heart.
You work for them, for those in factories, creaking with
silent dust, for those in workshops who are bending their backs.

Miklós Radnóti
translated from the Hungarian
by Stephen Berg, S.J. Marks,
and Steven Polgar

The Czar's Last Christmas Letter:
A Barn in the Urals

for Robert

You were never told, Mother, how old Illya was drunk
That last holiday, for five days and nights

He stumbled through Petersburg forming
A choir of mutes, he dressed them in pink ascension gowns

And, then, sold Father's Tirietz stallion so to rent
A hall for his Christmas recital: the audience

Was rowdy but Illya in his black robes turned on them
And gave them that look of his; the hall fell silent

And violently he threw his hair to the side and up
Went the baton—the recital ended exactly one hour

Later when Illya suddenly turned and bowed
And his mutes bowed, and what applause and hollering

Followed.
All of his cronies were there!

Illya told us later that he thought the voices
Of mutes combine in a sound

Like wind passing through big, winter pines.
Mother, if for no other reason I regret the war

With Japan for, you must now be told,
It took the servant, Illya, from us. *It was confirmed.*

He would sit on the rocks by the water and with his stiletto
Open clams and pop the raw meats into his mouth

And drool and laugh at us children.
We hear guns often, now, down near the village.

Don't think me a coward, Mother, but it is comfortable
Now that I am no longer Czar. I can take pleasure

From just a cup of clear water. I hear Illya's choir often.
I teach the children about decreasing fractions, that is

A lesson best taught by the father.
Alexandra conducts the French and singing lessons.

Mother, we are again a physical couple.
I brush out her hair for her at night.

She thinks that we'll be rowing outside Geneva
By the Spring. I hope she won't be disappointed.

Yesterday morning while bread was frying
In one corner, she in another washed all of her legs

Right in front of the children. I think
We became sad at her beauty. She has a purple bruise

On an ankle.
Like Illya I made her chew on mint.

Our Christmas will be in this excellent barn.
The guards flirt with your granddaughters and I see . . .

I see nothing wrong with it. Your little one, who is
Now a woman, made one soldier pose for her; she did

Him in charcoal, but as a bold nude. He was
Such an obvious virgin about it; he was wonderful!

Today, that same young man found us an enormous azure
And pearl samovar. Once, he called me Great Father

And got confused.
He refused to let me touch him.

I know they keep your letters from us. But, Mother,
The day they finally put them in my hands

I'll know that possessing them I am condemned
And possibly even my wife, and my children?

We will drink mint tea this evening.
Will each of us be increased by death?

With fractions as the bottom integer gets bigger, Mother, it
Represents less. That's the feeling I have about

This letter. I am at your request, The Czar.
And I am Nicholas.

Norman Dubie

NIGHT STRATEGIES

I kept brushing the cloth over the pouch of her stomach,
the cherubic and slightly chafed
folds of her hips,
remembering the voice rising off my radio,
a girl in Sarajevo, sixteen,
quivering between a translator and the thuds
of local shelling.

Just after dark she'd heard shouts in the street,
trash cans knocked over, panic
and the rumble of trucks,
and was crossing the room to blow out a lamp
when a soldier kicked in the door.

That dry wind in her throat,
what did it whisper about the authority of grief?

And when he pulled out of her,
when he buckled and holstered his pistol,
he went to the window and called in two comrades.
They left her naked on a bloody cot.
She wept, she said, but not inconsolably
like her mother, who clawed all night at the tiles
of their mosque.

I lathered the cloth with our wafer of soap
and dabbed at my daughter's stomach and thighs,
knowing the only answer I have
is this nervous

exaggeration of tenderness,
and that every ministry of my hand, clumsy
and apologetic, asks her
to practice such a radical faith.

David Bottoms

WORDS FOR MY DAUGHTER

About eight of us were nailing up forts
in the mulberry grove behind Reds's house
when his mother started screeching and
all of us froze except Reds—fourteen, huge
as a hippo—who sprang out of the tree so fast
the branch nearly bobbed me off. So fast,
he hit the ground running, hammer in hand,
and seconds after he got in the house
we heard thumps like someone beating a tire
off a rim   his dad's howls   the screen door
banging open   Saw   Reds barreling out
through the tall weeds toward the highway
the father stumbling after his fat son
who never looked back across the thick swale
of teazel and black-eyed susans until it was safe
to yell fuck you at the skinny drunk
stamping around barefoot and holding his ribs.

Another time, the Connelly kid came home to find
his alcoholic mother getting raped by the milkman.
Bobby broke a milk bottle and jabbed the guy
humping on his mom. I think it really happened
because none of us would loosely mention that
wraith of a woman who slippered around her house
and never talked to anyone, not even her kids.
Once a girl ran past my porch
with a dart in her back, her open mouth
pumping like a guppy's, her eyes wild.
Later that summer, or maybe the next,

the kids hung her brother from an oak.
Before they hoisted him, yowling and heavy
on the clothesline, they made him claw the creekbank
and eat worms. I don't know why his neck didn't snap.

Reds had another nickname you couldn't say
or he'd beat you up: "Honeybun."
His dad called him that when Reds was little.

*

So, these were my playmates. I love them still
for their justice and valor and desperate loves
twisted in shapes of hammer and shard.
I want you to know about their pain
and about the pain they could loose on others.
If you're reading this, I hope you will think,
Well, my dad had it rough as a kid, so what?
If you're reading this, you can read the news
and you know that children suffer worse.

*

Worse for me is a cloud of memories
still drifting off the South China Sea,
like the 9-year-old boy, naked and lacerated,
thrashing in his pee on a steel operating table
and yelling, *"Dau. Dau,"* while I, trying to translate
in the mayhem of Tet for surgeons who didn't know
who this boy was or what happened to him, kept asking
"Where? Where's the pain?" until a surgeon
said "Forget it. His ears are blown."

*

I remember your first Halloween
when I held you on my chest and rocked you,
so small your toes didn't touch my lap
as I smelled your fragrant peony head
and cried because I was so happy and because
I heard, in no metaphorical way, the awful chorus
of Sœur Anicet's orphans writhing in their cribs.
Then the doorbell rang and a tiny Green Beret
was saying trick-or-treat and I thought *oh oh*
but remembered it was Halloween and where I was.
I smiled at the evil midget, his map-light and night
paint, his toy knife for slitting throats, said,
"How ya doin', soldier?" and, still holding you asleep
in my arms, gave him a Mars Bar. To his father
waiting outside in fatigues I hissed, "You shit,"
and saw us, child, in a pose I know too well.

I want you to know the worst and be free from it.
I want you to know the worst and still find good.
Day by day, as you play nearby or laugh
with the ladies at Peoples Bank as we go around town
and I find myself beaming like a fool,
I suspect I am here less for your protection
than you are here for mine, as if you were sent
to call me back into our helpless tribe.

John Balaban

MARVELOUS FATHER

Slobodan Milosevic is a marvelous father.
He takes his children to the zoo every Sunday.
He turns his back on the snipers up in the hills
so his daughter can laugh at the little brown monkeys.
This is what we must strive for,
O friends, O villagers,
to be a zoo in the heart of a bombed-out city,
to be the whim of a girl with her hand on the gun,
the gun that is the man Radovan Karadzic,
the gun that is the man Franjo Tudjman,
the gun that is the hand named Hitler and Stalin,
devil twins of terror of 1945.
This is what we must strive for,
to be the snipers asleep above the insomniac town,
to be, every one of us, marvelous fathers,
to throw our children in the tanks as we splatter their enemies,
to throw our women in the wells—so what if they drown!
We must do it, do it, again and again
to the whores that are the wives of Slobodan Milosevic
who killed our chickens and our cows and drank all our vodka
O brothers, O friends!
This is what we must strive for!
To be the horsemen of plagues in the homes of the criminals,
to crush them like hawks and that lackey Mussolini,

to strafe them and bomb them like an American fist,
to be like MacArthur, like Lenin, like the Kaiser,
like Dracul the blood-eater with his stakes and his slaughter,
like your father, Haris, and *your* father, Marko—

We know they are such marvelous men.

Dana Levin

The Freight

Winter mornings I see
the ghost of my breath
when in my cold blue car
I turn the engine and slowly
back out of the garage,
looking over my shoulder
to see where I'm going.

My commute takes me south down Western
past car lots with white plastic banners
flapping like the wings of windblown gulls,
then down Peterson past the cemetery.
At Broadway there's always a traffic jam—
I sit awhile in the shadows of tall buildings.
But when I reach Lake Shore Drive, I race
along the ice-encrusted lake, rushing
through the middle years of life,
always anxious about being late.
Back and forth, every day:
my sweet rut.

This morning—
instead of turning in the direction of work—
on impulse
I went the opposite way,
driving north through falling snow
to the thrift store in Wilmette
to buy Andrew the bed
shaped like a race car—

a blue car with big, black wheels.
I'd seen it and wanted to be
there when the store doors opened.
I knew I'd have to pay,
carry the bed to the curb,
heave it to the roof and fasten it with ropes,
then drive home through deepening drifts,
wind buffeting my burdened car.
But I like thinking of him
sleeping in a race car,
the engine of his dreams and visions
carrying the freight of the soul,
and I've found that to make him happy
makes me forget my life.
Reconciled to being late—
snow falling heavier—
I drove home carefully,
going slow, his blue car
tied on top of my blue car,
one hand out the window, holding fast the ropes.

Richard Jones

"WE STARTED HOME, MY SON AND I"

We started home, my son and I.
Twilight already. The young moon
stood in the western sky and beside it
a single star. I showed them to my son
and explained how the moon should be greeted
and that this star is the moon's servant.
As we neared home, he said
that the moon is far, as far
as that place where we went.
I told him the moon is much, much farther
and reckoned: if one were to walk
ten kilometers each day, it would take
almost a hundred years to reach the moon.
But this was not what he wanted to hear.
The road was already almost dry.
The river was spread on the marsh; ducks and other waterfowl
crowed the beginning of night. The snow's crust
crackled underfoot—it must
have been freezing again. All the houses' windows
were dark. Only in our kitchen
a light shone. Beside our chimney, the shining moon,
and beside the moon, a single star.

Jaan Kaplinski
translated from the Estonian
by Kaplinski, Riina Tamm,
and Sam Hamill

SCOLDING MY SONS

My temples covered all in white, I'm
slack-muscled and loose-skinned for good

now. And though I do have five sons,
not one of them prizes paper and brush.

A-shu is already twice eight, and who's
ever equaled him for sheer laziness?

A-hsüan is fifteen, time studies began,
but he's immune to words and ideas.

Yung and Tuan are both thirteen now,
and they can't even add six and seven.

And T'ung-tzu, who's almost nine, does
nothing but forage pears and chestnuts.

If this is heaven's way, I'll offer it
that stuff in the cup. It needs a drink.

T'ao Ch'ien
translated from the Chinese
by David Hinton

Natural History

Late afternoon, autumn equinox,
and my daughter and I
are at the table, silently eating
fried eggs and muffins,
sharp cheese and yesterday's rice
warmed over.

We put our paper plates
in the woodstove and go outside:
sunlight fills the alders with
the geometries of long blond hair,
and twin ravens ride the roller coasters
of warm September air
out, toward Protection Island.

Together we enter the roughed-in room
beside our cabin and begin our chores together:
she, cutting and stapling insulation;
while I cut and nail tight rows of cedar.

We work in a silence broken only
by occasional banter. I wipe the cobwebs
from nooks and sills, working on my knees
as if this prayer of labor could save me,
as though the itch of fiberglass and sawdust
were an answer to some old incessant question
I never dare remember.

When evening comes at last,
cooling arms and faces, we stop
and stand back to assess our work together.

And I remember the face of my father
as he climbed down a long wooden ladder
thirty years before. He was a tall strong sapling
smelling of tar and leather, his pate bald
and burnt to umber by a sun
blistering the desert.

He strode those rows of coops
with a red cocker spaniel and tousled boy-child
at his heel. I turn to look
at my daughter: her mop of blond curls
catches the last trembling light of day.
Weary, her lean body sways.

Try as I might, I cannot remember
the wisdom of fourteen years, those pleasures
of discovery. Eron smiles. We wash up
at the woodstove as the sun dies into
a candle-flame. A light breeze rustles the first yellow leaves
of autumn as boughs slowly darken.
A squirrel, enraged, castigates the dog
for some inscrutable intrusion,
and Eron climbs the ladder to her loft.

Suddenly, I am utterly alone,
a child gazing up at his father, a father
smiling down on his daughter.

A strange shudder comes over me
like a chill. Is this what there is
to remember: long days roofing coops,
the building of rooms on a cabin, the in-
significant meal?

Shadows of moments mean everything
and nothing, the dying landscapes
of remembered human faces frozen
in a moment. My room
was in the basement, was knotty pine,
back there in diamondback country.

The night swings out over the cold Pacific.
I pour a cup of coffee, heavy in my bones.
Soon, this fine young woman
will stare into the eyes of her own son or daughter,
years blown suddenly behind her.

Will she remember only this ache,
the immense satisfaction of this longing?
May she be happy, filled with the essential,
working in the twilight, on her knees,
with her children, at autumn equinox,
gathering the stories of silence together,
preparing to greet the winter.

Sam Hamill

Poem

My little son comes running with open arms!
Sometimes I can't bear it,
Father.
Did I, too,
Open your heart almost to breaking?

Thomas McGrath

SON

Just after midnight, Andrew woke,
crying, struggling in the dark.
I lifted the tiny body from the crib,
whispered words of comfort.
But I could not console him.
He wanted to be held close
and rocked in his mother's arms.

Richard Jones

MOTHERS

In the still of night
Have we wept.
And our hearts, shattered and aching
Have prayed.
In the cold, cold moonlight
Have we sobbed
And dreamed of what might have been.
And our hearts have bled from stabs
Given unheeding.
We are the women who have suffered alone—
Alone and in silence.

Kay Boyle

SOR JUANA'S LAST DREAM

(an excerpt)

Be a child forever.

What my mother said
of her desire to see me
choose the cloistered life.
But I remember other
declarations—Mother and her
women friends agreeing:
There are women who have *children,*
and women who are *children.*

What kind of sentence, then,
is the one she formed at the
beginning of my convent life—
a curse? Perhaps a fantasy
unspeakable in the company of
women, like herself, who had been
sentenced fertile.

Gail Wronsky

Letter to an Absent Son

It's right to call you son. That cursing alcoholic
is the god I married early before I really knew him:
spiked to his crossbeam bed, I've lasted thirty years.
Nails are my habit now. Without them I'm afraid.

At night I spider up the wall to hide in crevices
deeper than guilt. His hot breath smokes me out.
I fall and fall into the arms I bargained for,
sifting them cool as rain. A flower touch could tame me.
Bring me down that giant beam to lie submissive
in his fumbling clutch. One touch. Bad weather
moves indoors, a cyclone takes me.

How shall I find a shelter in the clouds, driven by
gods, gold breaking out of them everywhere?
Nothing is what it pretends. It gathers to a loss
of leaves and graves. Winter in the breath.
Your father looked like you, his dying proportioned
oddly to my breast. I boxed him in my plain pine
arms and let him take his ease just for a minute.

Madeline DeFrees

THE FAMILY GROUP

That Sunday at the zoo I understood the child
I never had would look like this: stiff-fingered
spastic hands, a steady drool, and eyes in cages
with a danger sign. I felt like stone myself
the ancient line curved inward in a sunblind
stare. My eyes were flat. Flat eyes for tanned
young couples with their picture-story kids.

Heads turned our way but you'd learned not to care.
You stood tall as Greek columns, weather-streaked
face bent toward the boy. I wanted to take his hand,
hallucinate a husband. He whimpered at my touch.
You watched me move away and grabbed my other
hand as much in love as pity for our land-
locked town. I heard the visionary rumor of the sea.

What holds the three of us together in my mind
is something no one planned. The chiseled look of mutes.
A window shut to keep out pain. Wooden blank
of doors. That stance the mallet might surprise if it
could strike the words we hoard for fears galloping
at night over moors through convoluted bone.
The strange uncertain rumor of the sea.

Madeline DeFrees

I Sit

Down again.
This baby has
to be
weaned. Don't
bite, baby,
don't pull,
keep still, will
somebody get me
a glass of
water? All
right, baby,
so sweet,
look at that
brown eye
staring at me
over the curve
of my breast.

Susan Griffin

ON NURSING
for Janine

Distance laid its static on us as mothers
once we'd passed our rocky first spring together
phoning news ("Bad night." "Poop volcano!" "Mine woke
five times!"), the hours

we spent lonely pacing the kitchen, evenings
we had only howling warm tender bundled
weights, the phone, each other, and days we strolled through
Descanso Gardens.

On those paths of fallen, bruised camellias,
rolling shade and stone under wheels of strollers,
sleep-deprived, sore-nippled, confused and angry,
quipping, crying, we

shifted fussy small boys from tit to shoulder.
Sometimes I would pick up your tiny Mitchell,
gangly small anemone—eager grin, his
blue eyes darting. Sam

reared determination, back arched, neck stretched
toward his usurped position. On stone steps, we'd
change poops, trading stories of my best friend whose
first baby died in

labor, or your sister who arced milk at her
husband. Bought sprout sandwich and cookies from con-
cession; we'd plan on sharing but always went
back for seconds. I,

nursing, watched your son at your dewy nipples
and your blond hair beaded in orange sunlight,
watched your calves gain shape as months passed from labor—
I saw this wordless—

and I knew I loved your grown body fiercely
not unlike my love for those growing babies
and the guilty intimacy of tell-all
phone calls at midday.

As our babies started to stand and toddle,
your hurt marriage healed with your growing Mitchell.
Month by month our phone-calling dwindled out. My
problems continued.

Ah, Janine, time's passed. There have been such changes.
Sam starts preschool twice a week this September.
Sometimes I see boys who I think are Mitch— I'll
have no more babies.

Sometimes I remember Descanso Gardens—
missing noontimes spent at white plastic tables,
telling truths we couldn't share other places
to the shrill fugue of

birdcall, boy-call, soft urgent speech and nursing.
Underneath the clouds that would pass, the airplanes,
in the darting sun of that worn-down April,
our breasts grew firm, would

fill as Sam lay sleeping and Mitchell balanced
tiptoe on your lap. Then we itched and teared with
milk, skin stretched by holding. Like flood, or wind, the
pressure would drive our

speaking. How I wish I had known that baby
season (the days your Southern humor slipped and
saddened with the intimacy of marriage
broken, my whole life

emptied) that, 'Neen, without consent or words or
warning, in our melanin-darkened nipples,
milk entered, life claimed all those empty spaces in us; between us.

Jenny Factor

MOTHER AND SON

Still, in the stale cigarette smell
of motel rooms, I wake
if a child coughs next door, my palms
sweaty with impotent responsibility.
Tonight, home for a weekend,
you cough in the next room
sever my dreams and wake me
to frayed ends of the loosed cord.

3 a.m.
Turn on the light.
Read.

Seeing the light beneath my door
you wander in to sit on the end of the bed
and we are held an hour
in the lamp's circle
making a reef knot of our loose ends
until we slip from each other again
and, the light turned out,
drift separately into dawn.

Karen Swenson

THE GIFT

I was wrong when I compared the mask of my own face
to an artifact, some kind of relic, or the shed skin of a snake.
That day, there was no wounding. At the museum,
that morning, when the woman was teaching
the children how to make masks of their own faces
with the plaster-of-paris bandages that doctors use
for instant casts, I was glad to lather
my daughters' faces with lotion, to place the wet strips
on their faces, and later to feel on my own face,
the patting of their hands like the beating of eyelashes against
my cheeks. The fine grit of dissolved earth floating
on my skin was pleasant, cool, and, afterward, choosing
the colors to paint the mask was like selecting one's own
plumage: Ann's singular purple, Maria's
black and white splashed with orange, my turquoise.
When I was holding the shape of my own face in my hand,
it was nothing like a death mask. I saw how easy it was
to put the self aside and pick it up again. It wasn't the sacrificial mask
I'd seen in Mexico—a human skull inlaid with lapis lazuli, a
                                        merciless reduction—
but a moment of happiness, a fragile shell, the gift
of mother and daughters, when, laughing,
we shaped one another into being
by touching what we were.

Rebecca Seiferle

SEED

Corn is universal,
so like a Roman Senator.
Its truths are silk tassels.
True its ears are sometimes
rotten, impure.
But it aspires in vast acres,
rectangular spaces,
to conspire with every pollinator
and to bear for the future
in its yellow hair.

And what are your aspirations,
oh my dears,
who will wear into tatters
like the dry sheaves
left standing, stuttering
in November's wind;
my Indian corn, my maize,
my seeds for a ruined world.
Oh my daughters.

Ruth Stone

MOTHERS, DAUGHTERS

Through every night we hate,
preparing the next day's
war. She bangs the door.
Her face laps up my own
despair, the sour, brown eyes,
the heavy hair she won't
tie back. She's cruel,
as if my private meanness
found a way to punish us.

We gnaw at each other's
skulls. Give me what's mine.
I'd haul her back, choking
myself in her, herself
in me. There is a book
called *Poisons* on her shelf.
Her room stinks with incense,
animal turds, hamsters
she strokes like silk. They
exercise on the bathroom
floor, and two drop through
the furnace vent. The whole
house smells of the accident,
the hot skins, the small
flesh rotting. Six days
we turn the gas up then
to fry the dead. I'd fry
her head if I could until
she cried love, love me!

All she won't let me do.
Her stringy figure in
the windowed room shares
its thin bones with no one.
Only her shadow on the glass
waits like an older sister.
Now she stalks, leans forward,
concentrates merely on getting
from here to there. Her feet
are bare. I hear her breathe
where I can't get in. If I
break through to her, she will
drive nails into my tongue.

Shirley Kaufman

ANOTHER POEM FOR MOTHERS

Mother, I'm trying
to write
a poem to you—

which is how most
poems to mothers must
begin—or, *What I've wanted*

to say, Mother . . . but we
as children of mothers,
even when mothers ourselves,

cannot bear our poems
to them. Poems to
mothers make us feel

little again. How to describe
that world that mothers spin
and consume and trap

and love us in, that spreads
for years and men and miles?
Those particular hands that could

smooth anything. butter on bread,
cool sheets or weather. It's
the wonder of them, good or bad,

those mother-hands that pet
and shape and slap,
that sew you together

the pieces of a better house
or life in which you'll try
to live. Mother,

I've done no better
than the others, but for now,
here is your clever failure.

Erin Belieu

CIGARETTES

my father burned us all. ash
fell from his hand onto our beds,
onto our tables and chairs.
ours was the roof the sirens
rushed to at night
mistaking the glow of his pain
for flame. nothing is burning here,
my father would laugh, ignoring
my charred pillow, ignoring his own
smoldering halls.

Lucille Clifton

Two, Hers and Mine

I had a child who delighted me
everyday her growth
and grown she has become
wondrously forgiving
to all my errors that worked
in her life like thorns
giving us both a time
of rusty pain, for me
thrown back again to
infancy and all
that was done to me, the
harshest music of that truth
played out in lives
two, hers and mine
leaping as you could not have thought
quicker than the eye.

Susan Griffin

THE CABBAGE

You have rented an apartment.
You come to this enclosure with physical relief,
your heavy body climbing the stairs in the dark,
the hall bulb burned out, the landlord
of Greek extraction and possibly a fatalist.
In the apartment leaning against one wall,
your daughter's painting of a large frilled cabbage
against a dark sky with pinpoints of stars.
The eager vegetable, opening itself
as if to eat the air, or speak in cabbage
language of the meanings within meanings;
while the points of stars hide their massive
violence in the dark upper half of the painting.
You can live with this.

Ruth Stone

A Grandfather's Last Letter

Elise, I have your valentine with the red shoes. I have
Waited too many weeks to write—wanting to describe
The excitement on the back lawn for you:

                                    the forsythia

Is now a bright yellow, and with the ribbons you draped
Inside it, trembles in a breeze,
All yellow and blues, like that pilot light this winter
Worried by just a little breath that came out of you.

On the dark side of the barn there's the usual railing
Of snow.
The tawny owl, nightingales, and moles
Have returned to the lawn again.

I have closed your grandmother's front rooms.

I know you miss her too. Her crocus bed showed its first
Green nose this morning. For breakfast I had
A duck's egg and muffins.

Your father thinks I shouldn't be alone?
Tell him I have planted a row of volunteer radishes.
I have replaced the north window . . .

So you have read your first book. Sewed a dress for
The doll. The very young and old are best at finding
Little things to do. The world is jealous of us, you know?

The moles are busy too. Much more mature this year,
The boar with the black velvet coat made a twelve-
Foot-long gallery under the linden where the mockingbirds
Are nesting.

The moles took some of my rags to add to
Their nursery of grass, leaves, and roots.
The cream-colored sow is yet to make her appearance!
They have seven mounds. Each with three bolt doors
Or holes. The pine martens are down from the woods, I see them
In the moonlight waiting for a kill.

Molehills can weaken a field so that a train
Passing through it sinks suddenly, the sleepers
In their berths sinking too!

I wonder what it's like in their underground rooms:
Their whiskers telegraphing the movements
Of earthworms. They don't require water when on
A steady diet of night crawlers. Worms are almost
Entirely made of water.

Last night there was quite an incident. The sun was going
Down and the silly boar was tunneling toward
The linden and he went shallow, the owl dropped down
Setting its claws into the lawn, actually taking hold
Of the blind mole, at that moment the mockingbird,
Thinking her nest threatened, fell on the owl putting
Her tiny talons into his shoulders. Well,

There they were, Elise, the owl on top of the invisible
Mole, the mockingbird on top of the owl. The mole

Moved backward a foot,
The birds were helpless and moved with him.
They formed quite a totem. The two birds looked so serious
In their predicament. A wind brushed the wash on the line.
And our three friends broke each for its respective zone.

Tomorrow the vines on the house are coming down. I want
The warmth of the sun on that wall. I'm sending
You a package with some of your grandmother's old clay
Dolls, silverware, and doilies.

Tell your father he is not coming in June to kill
The moles! Tell him to go fishing instead, or to take
Your mother to Florida.

You said you worry that someday I'll be dead also! Well,
Elise, of course, I will. I'll be hiding then from your world
Like our moles. They move through their tunnels
With a swimming motion. They don't know where they're going—

But they go.

There's more to this life than we know. If ever
You're sleeping in a train on the northern prairies
And everything sinks a little
But keeps on going, then, you've visited me in another world—

Where I am going.

Norman Dubie

After Tomasito's Departure

The sun still shines,
And the moon moves on the waters.
In the heavy press of the heat,
The flowers and the citizens shrivel.
Everything in order for the summer solstice:

But the whole city empty—
Since you've been gone.

Thomas McGrath

NOTES TO MY DAUGHTERS

You were the reason for staying.
It's always the children who leave,
not the mother. It was the end
of winter, isn't that always
the best time. Freesias suddenly
out of the mud, little milk teeth,
plum trees unbuttoned and the sky
on the Bayshore freeway to the airport
lined with blue tile.

Do you feel abandoned,
now you are women?

*

From the ridge of our mountain
we can see the Judean wilderness
slide to the bottom of the world.

Sometimes the parched air ripples
with dust as if everyone's beating
carpets and the shudder of wind
is like nervous laughter out of the caves.

It's all getting smaller and farther.
The earth wears a thin green fuzz
where the sheep graze
stubby in the distance as if
they were cut out and pasted there.

*

I've learned what he knows,
how to tell sonic booms from the others.
To mean what we say.

First thing in the morning
in the Valley of the Cross
when the night is still drying
on the leaves and the red poppies
stand up straight
as if pulled by strings,

a man balances on his head
in the wet grass, we're behind
two Ethiopian joggers
and a woman walking her boxer.

The rest of it empty
like the future no one plans for.

*

There's an overwrought smell of jasmine,
tiny wax flowers, wiry stems
around the railing of our balcony.
Too tame to fly, the vines
catch on and keep climbing.

Scent of my old life, where the light
falls back of my shoulders
into your day.

*

If not for the three of you, if not
for the two of us,
if not for my cousin's strawberry jam
at breakfast and a woodpecker
attacking our jacaranda
outside the kitchen window, drilling
so loud we don't hear
the seven o'clock news, if not
for persimmons and the first
green oranges we wait for
and the small hard peaches
that arrive in the market in April,
if not for the ripening
when we expect it, bulbs
of new garlic spread out to dry
just when the old garlic's rotting,
if not for Mary's latest recipes,
meat loaf with carrots and cumin
and fennel soup, and Mussa's
bottles of green-gold oil
from his olive trees in Beit Safafa,
and the crested larks, little tan females
singing their hearts out on both sides
of the green line, if not for
the bulbul's five purple eggs,
and all the glad birds on Yom Kippur
praising the parked cars
in the empty streets and the prayers
of the ones who keep praying,
if not for the archaeologist unlocking
the safe in the museum to show us

the yellowed bone, the rusty nail
still hammered through the heel,
if not for the gilded dome and the silver dome
balloons and bells
and the muezzin calling, peace
marches around the Old City wall and me
on the ramparts following my body,
if not for the two of us, waves
of white surf breaking
over the hawthorn's arthritic limbs,
if not for what flickers as joy
in the middle of grieving,
what could I say when you ask me
whether I'm happy.

*

One day I'll look up at the hills
and they won't be there. Lately
I think about my death.
It keeps me connected to the world.

I wonder if you'll come
to put little stones on me
the way Jews do to keep the unliving
where they belong.

*

I wish I could learn how
to strike matches in the wind
so they won't go out in my cupped hand.
I wish I could peel an orange
in one long ribbon that doesn't break.
I wish you were with me
in this hard land waiting for the first rain
after a long dry season
when the sky tilts and spills over
making a fresh start,
stirring the dust into muddy trickles,
clearing everything but not
washing it away.

Shirley Kaufman

CHILDREN

What good are children anyhow?
       They only break your heart.
The one that bore your fondest hopes
       will never amount to anything.
The one you slaved to give the chances you never had
       rejects them with contempt.
They won't take care of you in your old age.
       They don't even write home.
They don't follow in your footsteps.
They don't avoid your mistakes.
It's impossible to save them from pain.
       And of course they never listen.

Remember how you hung on the lips
       of your father or grandfather,
Begging for the old stories:
       "Again! Tell it again!
       What was it like 'in olden times'?"
We have good stories too:
       funny, instructive, pathetic.
Forget it. Write them down for your friends.
Your friends, with whom you have that unspoken pact:
Don't ask me about my children, and I won't inquire of yours.

Remember how we used to exchange infant pictures?
How we boasted of cute sayings? How we . . .
       Forget it.
Put away those scrapbooks, with the rusted flute in the closet,
       with the soiled ballet slippers.

Tear up the clumsy Valentines.
Tear up every crayoned scrap that says, "I love you, Mama."
They don't want us to keep these mementos:
      they find them embarrassing,
These relics of dependent love,
The orange crayon that didn't dare write, "I hate you."
Forget their birthdays, as they forget yours.

Perhaps because they never finish anything,
      not a book, not a school,
Their politics are cruel and sentimental:
Some monster of depravity
      who destroyed millions with his smile,
Who shadowed our youth with terror,
      is a hero to them.
Now he smiles benignly from their walls.

Because they are historyless, they don't believe in history:
      Stalin wasn't so bad.
      The Holocaust didn't really happen.
      Roosevelt was a phony.
But the worst of it is:
      they don't believe we ever believed;
They don't believe we ever had ideals.
They don't believe that we were ever poor.
They don't believe that we were passionate
      —or that we are passionate today!
Forget it. Don't torture yourself.
      You still have some life to salvage.
Get divorced. Go on a diet.
Take up the career you dropped for them twenty years ago.

Go back to the schools they deserted, and sign up for courses:
Study Tranquility 101; take Meditation; enroll for Renewal.

Remember those older friends we used to envy,
       brilliant and glittering with beauty,
Who refused to have children,
       not about to sacrifice their careers;
Who refused the mess, the entrapment,
       as we toiled over chores and homework,
       worried about measles and money—
Have you seen them lately?
They no longer converse in sparkling cadenzas.
They are obsessed with their little dog
       who piddles on the Oriental rug,
       who throws up on the bedspread.

They don't notice his bad breath;
His incessant yapping doesn't seem to disturb them.
To be honest about it,
       the whole apartment smells!
And the way they babble to him in pet names
       instead of talk of Milton, Chaucer, Dante.
The way they caress him makes you fairly ill;
       the way they call him, "Baby."

Carolyn Kizer

THE CONDITION OF WOMEN

Sisters, do you know how it is? On one hand,
the bawling baby; on the other, your husband

sliding onto your stomach,
his little son still howling at your side.

Yet, everything must be put in order.
Rushing around all helter-skelter.

Husband and child, what obligations!
Sisters, do you know how it is?

Hồ Xuân Hương
translated from the Vietnamese
by John Balaban

Yesterday

My friend says I was not a good son
you understand
I say yes I understand

he says I did not go
to see my parents very often you know
and I say yes I know

even when I was living in the same city he says
maybe I would go there once
a month or maybe even less
I say oh yes

he says the last time I went to see my father
I say the last time I saw my father

he says the last time I saw my father
he was asking me about my life
how I was making out and he
went into the next room
to get something to give me

oh I say
feeling again the cold
of my father's hand the last time

he says and my father turned
in the doorway and saw me
look at my wristwatch and he

said you know I would like you to stay
and talk with me

oh yes I say

but if you are busy he said
I don't want you to feel that you
have to
just because I'm here

I say nothing

he says my father
said maybe
you have important work you are doing
or maybe you should be seeing
somebody I don't want to keep you

I look out the window
my friend is older than I am
he says and I told my father it was so
and I got up and left him then
you know

though there was nowhere I had to go
and nothing I had to do

W.S. Merwin

THE STORM

I called my father long-distance last night
to let him know how we're doing—
Andrew feeling much better, the baby kicking,
me taking a turn with the flu, feeling like
I'm inside a glass bubble. My father patiently
waited for me to finish what I was saying,
then eagerly told me about the terrible
thunderstorm, asking if I could hear
the rain beating down. Suddenly
neither of us was talking.
I stood with the phone to my ear,
listening to drumming on the skylight
in my father's kitchen, picturing an old man
holding the receiver up to the thunder and darkness.

Richard Jones

LAST WILL AND TESTAMENT

for Tomasito

Son,
Forgive me:
When you were little,
I made some money,
Once,
And saved it
For what they call
Your "future"
And,
Alas,
I did it without
Robbing a bank.

Forgive me, son
(And all other children), that,
One time,
I made an agreement with
The enemy.

Thomas McGrath

WHY YOUR FATHER CRIED

Your sister is telling the story. It was
June, the year he died. They are on
the porch. The wisteria curves around,
making what is said seem a secret. Your father
is an old man. There is so much to remember.
She can see that he is crying. How can she not
feel sad, somewhat peripheral? She is beside him
but a memory of you has kindled him to tears.
You had a paper route. You got up in the dark.
Snow might be falling. Your squat, little boy's
hands rolled and twisted the papers into logs
that you piled in the basket of your bike.
Then you buttoned your heavy coat. All your motions
carried the stiffness of sleep and inexperience.
Your father stood watching from a doorway. He wanted
to go to you and stop you, to send you back
to bed. He'd take the papers for you in his car.
But no, regret would be a door to duty. He let you go.

Your mother, who has been pouring tea, looks up.
"It wasn't you," she says. "Of course, he loved you
awfully well. But he was crying for himself."
She is thinking how his mother must have felt,
waking him for work, nudging him into a consciousness
of six younger brothers and sisters. She passes
the thin china cups. Grains of rice are fired into them
where the light shines through. Their bottoms
and rims and the underlying saucers all are edged
with a pattern like blue bridges, like the letter "H"

circling around. You pick yours up and hold it
toward you, drinking. Maybe you see the word "I"
pointing to you many times, "I," "I," "I," "I," and so
you speak. "Couldn't he see that I wanted to go—
under my own steam—away from the house
and what he gave me? I wonder what I was thinking,
out, like that, in the dark. I know they were
some of the best thoughts I had in my life."

Elaine Terranova

BORN INTO A WORLD KNOWING

This will happen
Oh god we say just give
me a few more
breaths
and don't let it be
terrible
let it be soft
perhaps in someone's
arms, perhaps tasting
chocolate
perhaps
laughing or asking
Is it over already?
or saying *not yet. Not*
yet the sky
has at this moment turned
another shade of blue,
and see there a child
still plays
in the fresh snow.

Susan Griffin

I Thought Back and

There I was
at the top of the walnut tree
in my old red sweater
my dress catching on twigs
my legs scratched from climbing.
Wind bent the boughs
almost to breaking:

Growing in every cell
I never once thought of you
thinking about me.

Your problem is forever looking
backward.
All you see is me
waiting for the next big
noisy gust of wind
to hang from.

All you see is me
not thinking of you,
old woman,
me singing.

Ann Stanford

ENDING WITH A LINE FROM *LEAR*

I will try to remember. It was light.
It was also dark, in the grave. I could feel
how dark it was, how black it would be
without my father. When he was gone.
But he was not gone, not yet. He was only
a corpse, and I could still touch him
that afternoon. Earlier the same afternoon.
This is the one thing that scares me:
losing my father. I don't want him to go.
I am a young man. I will never be older.
I am wearing a tie and a watch. The sky,
gray, hangs over everything. Today
the sky has no curve to it, and no end.
He is deep into his mission. He has business
to attend to. He wears a tie but no watch.
I will skip a lot of what happens next.
Then the moment comes. Everything, everything
has been said, and the wheels start to turn.
They roll, the straps unwind, and the coffin
begins to descend. Into the awful damp.
Into the black center of the earth. I
am being left behind. The center of my body
sinks down into the cold fire of the grave.
But still my feet stand on top of the dirt.
My father's grave. I will never again.
Never. Never. Never. Never. Never.

Marvin Bell

SHE CAME TO SAY FAREWELL

On the day after her death
mother came
to say farewell to me.

At night I heard
her steps nearing my bed
step
by step. She stopped
by my head.

I said: Mommy,
do not appear, Mommy,
my heart will burst
from fear.

No more than that
I said to her
by way of farewell.

Anna Swir
translated from the Polish
by Czesław Miłosz and Leonard Nathan

PROVENANCE

I want to tell you the story of that winter
in Madrid where I lived in a room
with no windows, where I lived
with the death of my father, carrying it
everywhere through the streets,
as if it were an object, a book written
in a luminous language I could not read.
Every day I left my room and wandered
across the great plazas of that city,
boulevards crowded with people and cars.
There was nowhere I wanted to go.
Sometimes I would come to myself
inside a cathedral under the vaulted
ceiling of the transept, I would find
myself sobbing, transfixed in the light
slanting through the rose window
scattering jewels across the cold
marble floor. At this distance now
the grief is not important, nor the sadness
I felt day after day wandering the maze
of medieval streets, wandering the rooms
of the Prado, going from painting
to painting, looking into Velázquez,
into Bosch, Brueghel, looking for something
that would help, that would frame
my spirit, focus sorrow into some
kind of belief that wasn't fantasy
or false, for I was tired of deception,
the lies of words, even the Gypsy violin,

its lament with the *puñal* inside
seemed indulgent, posturing.
I don't mean to say these didn't
move me, I was an easy mark,
anything could well up in me—
rainshine on the cobblestone streets,
a bowl of tripe soup in a peasant café.
In my world at that time there was
no scale, nothing with which
to measure, I could no longer
discern value—the mongrel eating
scraps of garbage in the alley
was equal to *Guernica* in all its
massive outrage. When I looked
in the paintings mostly what I saw
were questions. In the paradise
panel of *The Garden of Earthly Delights*
why does Bosch show a lion
disemboweling a deer? Or that man
in hell crucified on the strings of a harp?
In his *Allegory of the Seven Deadly Sins*:
Gluttony, Lust, Sloth, Wrath, Envy, Avarice,
Pride—of which am I most guilty?
Why in Juan de Flanders' *Resurrection
of Lazarus* is the face of Christ so sad
in bringing the body back to life?
Every day I returned to my room,
to my cave where I could not look out
at the world, where I was forced into
the one place I did not want to be. In
the Cranach painting—behind Venus

with her fantastic hat, her cryptic look,
behind Cupid holding a honeycomb, whimpering
with bee stings—far off in the background,
that cliff rising above the sea, that small hut
on top—is that Cold Mountain, is that where
the poet made his way out of our world?
My father had little use for poems, less use
for the future. If he had anything
to show me by his life, it was to live
here. Even in a room without windows.
One day in the Prado, in the Hall
of the Muses, a group of men
in expensive suits, severe looking,
men of importance, with a purpose,
moved down the hallway toward me,
and I was swept aside, politely,
firmly. As they passed I glimpsed
in their midst a woman, in a simple
black dress with pearls, serene, speaking
to no one, and then she and the men
were gone. *Who was that?* I asked,
and a guard answered: *The Queen.*
The Queen. In my attempt to follow
to see which painting she would choose,
I got lost in one of the Goya rooms
and found myself before one of his
dark paintings, one from his last years
when the world held no more illusions,
where love was examined in a ruthless,
savage anger. In this painting
a woman stood next to Death, her beauty,

her elegance, her pearls and shining hair
meant nothing in His presence,
and He was looking out from the painting,
looking into me, and Death took my hand
and made me look, and I saw my own face
streaming with tears, and the day
took on the shape of a crouching beast,
and my father's voice called out in wonder
or warning, and every moment
I held on made it that much harder
to let go, and Death demanded
that I let go. Then the moment
disappeared, like a pale horse, like
a ghost horse disappearing deep inside
Goya's painting. I left the Prado.
I walked by the *Palacio Real* with its
2,000 rooms, one for every kind
of desire. I came upon the *Rastro,*
the great open-air bazaar, a flea market
for the planet, where everything in the world
that has been cast aside, rejected, lost,
might be found, where I found Cervantes,
an old, dusty copy of *Don Quixote,*
and where I discovered an old mirror,
and looking into it found my father's face
in my face looking back at me,
and behind us a Brueghel world
crowded with the clamor of the market,
people busy with their lives, hunting,
searching for what's missing. How casual
they seemed, in no hurry, as if they had all

of time, no frenzy, no worry,
as the Castilian sun made its slow
arch over us, the same sun
that lanced the fish on crushed ice
in the market stalls, fish with open mouths,
glazed stares, lapped against each other
like scales, by the dozens, the *Madrileños*
gaping over them, reading them
like some sacred text, like some kind
of psalm or prophecy as they made
their choice, and had it wrapped in paper,
then disappeared into the crowd.
And that is all. I wanted to tell you
the story of that winter in Madrid
where I lived in a room with no windows
at the beginning of my life without my father.
When the fascist officials asked Picasso
about *Guernica*: "Are you responsible
for this painting?" He looked back
at them, and answered slowly: "No.
You are." What should I answer
when asked about this poem?
I wanted to tell you the story of that winter
in Madrid, where my father kept dying, again
and again, inside of me, and I kept
bringing him back, holding him for as long
as I could. I never knew how much
I loved him. I didn't know that grief

would give him back to me, over
and over, I didn't know that those
cobbled streets would someday
lead to here, to this quietude,
this blessing, to my father
within me.

Joseph Stroud

IF I LEAVE YOU

for Joaquín

Heaven has once again become valuable to me.
Somewhere along, I lost it

And I'm not saying I've found it again.
But I have a son now and he's almost six.

He's the one who needs it.
Or maybe he doesn't.

Six-year-olds do pretty good
Without any help from me.

I guess I'm saying it's me—
I am the one who needs it, but for him.

I need heaven again
So that I've got something to say,

The same way I needed something said to me
About dog heaven

And every other time
There was nothing else to say.

In those moments there's a heaven somewhere
Inside the word itself,

And maybe that's all
There needs to be.

What it is,
Is that there needs to be something.

It's that uncomplicated.
There needs to be something

And I need to be able to say it
When my boy looks at me

And when I look back at him.
I need this word,

And he needs me to have it
When he talks about his grandfather

Or Aunt Connie
Or six-toed Hector the Pal-Cat we had forever.

It's not bigger than that,
And it's not smaller.

It's a nothing jump from there
To guardian angels,

To the picture from my bedroom,
The picture that became part of the wall

After so many years. You know which one:
Two kids crossing a bridge,

High up in some kind of mountains,
The two of them almost ready to fall

Off the rickety planks, and no parents anywhere.
Just the green angel,

Big and happy-eyed and watching them
So that I felt better

Looking at it in the dark
As I got myself ready

To go to sleep,
Wherever Sleep was.

Going to sleep:
It sounded like going somewhere—

Away from home
And by myself—

To the terror I see now
My parents must have harbored

Every time
I started out,

Just the way I feel it when my son lies down.
Just the way

The only thing I can do
For My Little and Good Man

Is pack him a lunch of heaven
For the trail,

Heaven and angels
And gold-talk—something

To carry him along
When I can't be there.

It's all I can do and it isn't much
And it's all that was done for me.

I've got a couple of words for him.
And that's it.

That's all he can carry.

It's nothing to jump further, as well,
To growing up small-town:

Unlocked doors,
And the time I shocked my parents

Because I saw their eyes get so big—
I'll tell you—

When I told them
I wanted to be a priest.

It wasn't true exactly;
It was just the fifties.

I was in catechism.
The space race was on,

And in our nun's classroom
A bulletin board marked attendance

By everybody having a paper spaceship
She moved up one big planet toward God

Each Thursday you came here after school.
I wanted to get to heaven first.

It was a strange goal,
All of us still being alive

And fifth-graders like we were.

I don't know if I believe in heaven.
It's true I need it.

This is a funny thing
To hear myself say.

Maybe that nun was right.
Maybe you needed heaven

Right in the classroom,
And when you are alive

And not just dead.
I can't believe she was right,

And I don't want to.
I don't believe

She gave me the answer to anything else,
Not even what happened

To the ark of the covenant,
Which became my favorite question that year

Because nobody could answer it
Until they made the Indiana Jones movies

And then all I wanted to say was,
I thought of this plot first.

But wearing a scapular,
Making first Communion, that stuff,

It all just got in the way, finally,
And getting dressed up

In good clothes on Sundays—
And then for anything—

Just made me get sick in my stomach.
I still feel that way, mostly.

I don't know when I really learned
Anything about heaven,

Or if I did learn anything
Not already on a postcard

Or a calendar.
But there you are.

I've got a little boy now,
Just the way I was a little boy,

And I don't know what else to do.

Alberto Ríos

COMICE

I think of Issa often these days, his poems about the loneliness
of fleas, watermelons becoming frogs to escape from thieves.
Moon in solstice, snowfall under the earth, I dream of a pure life.
Issa said of his child, *She smooths the wrinkles from my heart.*
Yes, it's a dewdrop world. Inside the pear there's a paradise
we will never know, our only hint the sweetness of its taste.

Joseph Stroud

Not Writing Poems about Children

Once I gave birth to living metaphors.
Not poems now, Ben Jonson, they became themselves.

In despair of poetry, which had fled away,
From loops and chains of children, these were let grow:

"The little one is you all over . . ."
They fulfill their impulses, not mine.

They invent their own categories,
Clear and arbitrary. No poem needs them.

They need only what they say:
"When I grow up I'm going to marry a tree."

Children do not make up for lost occasions—
"You'd rather kiss that poem than kiss me."

Creation halts, for denials and embraces,
Assurances that no poem replaces them,

Nor, as you knew, Ben, holds the mirror to them,
Nor consoles the parent-artist when they go.

Poems only deprive us of our loss
(Deliberate sacrifice to a cold stanza)

If Art is more durable to us than children,
Or if we, as artists, are more durable than our love.

Ben, I hope you wrote about your dead son
While you were tranced with pain,

Did not offer up those scenes of the infant Isaac in your mind
For the greater poem; but emerged from that swoon

Clutching a page some stranger might have written;
Like a condolence note, cursorily read and tossed aside.

Perhaps at this extremity, nothing improves or worsens.
Talent irrelevant. No poems in stones.

For once, you do not watch yourself
At a desk, covering foolscap. Denied the shameful relief

Of actors, poets, nubile female creatures,
Who save tears like rainwater, for rinsing hair, and mirrors.

Finally, we are left alone with poems,
Children that we cling to, or relinquish

For their own sakes. The metaphor, like love,
Springs from the very separateness of things.

Carolyn Kizer

WE HAVE KNOWN

We have known such joy as a child knows.
My sons, in whom everything rests,
know that there were those who were deeply
in love, and who asked you in,
and who did not claim a tree of thoughts
like family branches would sustain you.

My sons, in whom I am well pleased,
you will learn that a man is not a child,
and there is that which a woman cannot bear,
but as deep wounds for which you may hate
me, who must live in you a long time,
coursing abrasively in the murky passages.

These poems, also, are such and such passages
as I have had to leave you. If very little
can pass through them, know that I did,
and made them, and finally did not need them.
We have known such joys as a child knows,
and will not survive, though you have them.

Marvin Bell

Time, Place, and Parenthood

Here we are, my son, aliens in this place
That seems so remote from our origin among
The superb slopes and deep valleys of the Green
Mountains, only a day's drive to the east.
Most people nowadays think aliens
Must come from Mars, and indeed sometimes
I feel remarkably Martian, so apparent
Are even the little distinctions of time and place
To me in my old age. And sometimes also
You now in your maturity of body and mind,
Your handsome strength, seem so distinct from
The four-year-old boy who rode beside me
In our pickup over the mountains, or the six-
Year-old who built the hut under the roots
Of the half-washed-out hemlock by the brook,
That I can recall you only as in a faded
Photograph from another country. But no,
It isn't true, not for more than an instant. I still
Remember you clinging in my arms as we ran
Down the tilt of Marshall's pasture, or holding
My hand as we entered the little post office
In our old town, so loving, so loyal. In these,
My son, you have been constant; almost four
Decades later you are the same. My son—
My Bo, my David—my man now in this world—
Accept these words that can never say enough.

Hayden Carruth

CELEBRATION

How wonderful, Tomasito!
All of us here!
Together . . .
A little while
On the road through . . .

Thomas McGrath

About the Poets

Every Copper Canyon Press book exists to serve the poem. We can only do this with the support of our poets. The poems in this volume have been drawn from past and future Copper Canyon Press books and we gratefully acknowledge and thank the follwing poets for permission to use their work in this anthology:

JOHN BALABAN is the author of *Locusts at the Edge of Summer: New & Selected Poems* and translator of *Spring Essence: The Poetry of Hồ Xuân Hương*. During the American war in Vietnam, Balaban performed alternative service duty, first as a teacher and later as a volunteer working to bring war-injured children out of Vietnam for better medical care. His collection of Vietnamese folk poetry, *Ca Dao Vietnam,* is forthcoming from Copper Canyon Press. His daughter is Tally.

ERIN BELIEU is the author of *Infanta* and *One Above & One Below*. She has written poetry about her son, Jude, since his birth in 2001.

MARVIN BELL's most recent collection is *Nightworks: Poems 1962–2000*. A longtime professor at the Writers' Workshop at the University of Iowa, he is Iowa's Poet Laureate. A constant traveler, with his wife, Dorothy, he divides his time between Iowa City, Port Townsend, and Long Island. Their sons are Nathan Saul Bell and Jason Aaron Bell, and their grandchildren are Colman Saul Bell and Aileen Violet Bell. His poem "Ending with a Line from *Lear*" refers to the scene in Shakespeare's play where Lear is looking upon the corpse of his daughter Cordelia.

STEPHEN BERG is an editor and founder of *American Poetry Review.* His books include *New & Selected Poems, The Steel Cricket: Versions 1958–1997,* and *Crow with No Mouth: Ikkyū*. His daughters are Clair and Margot.

DAVID BOTTOMS is the author of *Vagrant Grace* and *Armored Hearts: Selected & New Poems,* and is Georgia's Poet Laureate. His forthcoming book is *Vigilance.* His daughter is Rachel.

KAY BOYLE was born in St. Paul, Minnesota, in 1902 and began her writing life in Paris during the 1920s, publishing in the expatriate magazine *transition,* and becoming friends with Djuna Barnes, Samuel Beckett, James Joyce, and other writers and artists. After World War II she was a foreign correspondent for *The New Yorker,* and went on to publish more than two dozen books of fiction, poetry, translations, and essays, including *Collected Poems of Kay Boyle.*

HAYDEN CARRUTH is the author of dozens of collections of poetry and prose, including *Doctor Jazz* and *Scrambled Eggs & Whiskey: Poems 1991–1995,* which won the 1996 National Book Award in Poetry. He is the father of Martha and David, also known as "the Bo." His long poem "Dearest M" is an elegy for Martha.

LUCILLE CLIFTON is the author of *the book of light.* She is a recipient of the National Book Award in Poetry, and is presently Distinguished Professor of Humanities at St. Mary's College of Maryland.

MADELINE DEFREES entered the convent in 1935 and left it thirty-eight years later. Her book *Blue Dusk: New & Selected Poems* surveys a fifty-year career of writing and publishing poetry. A student of Karl Shapiro, John Berryman, and Robert Fitzgerald, Madeline DeFrees has taught and inspired countless writers through the writing programs at the University of Montana and the University of Massachusetts.

GERARDO DENIZ is the pen name of Juan Almela. This poem, translated by Mónica de la Torre, is reprinted from *Reversible Monuments: Contemporary Mexican Poetry,* and from Deniz's *Poemas/Poems,* published in the United States by Lost Roads Publishers. Deniz and Almela live in Mexico City with Koshka, his beloved cat and sole living creature with whom he has shared his daily life for more than thirteen years.

NORMAN DUBIE is the author of *The Mercy Seat: Collected & New Poems 1967–2001*. His daughter is Hannah and his granddaughter is Kaya.

JENNY FACTOR is the author of *Unraveling at the Name,* winner of the 2001 Hayden Carruth Award. Her son is Lev.

SUSAN GRIFFIN is the author of *Bending Home: Selected & New Poems 1967–1998.*

SAM HAMILL is the author and translator of dozens of books of poetry, including *Destination Zero* (White Pine Press), *Dumb Luck* and *Gratitude* (BOA Editions). He is the founding editor of Copper Canyon Press and occasionally writes under the nom de plume Obaka the Pilgrim. His daughter is Eron.

HÔ XUÂN HƯƠNG was a nineteenth-century Vietnamese poet whose work is revered in Vietnam. Not much is known about her life, except that she was a concubine who ran a tea shop and gained fame for the cleverness and wit of her poems. Her poetry appears in *Spring Essence: The Poetry of Hô Xuân Hương,* translated by John Balaban.

RICHARD JONES is the author of *The Blessing: New and Selected Poems.* He lives in Chicago with his wife, Laura, and their sons Andrew and William. Andrew has moved on to a bunk bed, and William now dreams in a blue car.

JAAN KAPLINSKI lives in Estonia and is the author of *The Wandering Border* and *The Same Sea in Us All* (Breitenbush Books). He translated his own work, with the help of Sam Hamill and Riina Tamm.

SHIRLEY KAUFMAN grew up in Seattle and lived for many years in San Francisco, before immigrating to Israel in 1973. She lives in Jerusalem with her husband, William Daleski. Her daughters are Sharon, Joan, and Deborah. Her most recent books are *Roots in the Air: New & Selected Poems* and the forthcoming *Threshold.*

CAROLYN KIZER is the Pulitzer Prize—winning author of *Cool, Calm & Collected: Poems 1960–2000* and *Harping On*. She lives in Sonoma, California.

DANA LEVIN is the author of *In the Surgical Theatre,* which won the 1999 *American Poetry Review*/Honickman First Book Prize.

CLARENCE MAJOR is the author of *Configurations: New & Selected Poems 1958–1998,* nominated for a National Book Award in 1999. His forthcoming book is *Waiting for Sweet Betty.*

THOMAS MCGRATH was born on a North Dakota farm in 1916 and died in Minneapolis in 1990. His books include *Selected Poems: 1938–1988* and *Death Song.* His many small poems written for his son, Tomasito, are matched in their beauty by his masterful epic, *Letter to an Imaginary Friend.*

W.S. MERWIN lives in Haiku, Hawaii, and is the author of *The First Four Books of Poems, The Second Four Books of Poems, Flower & Hand,* and *East Window,* among many other volumes of poetry. His translations of Jean Follain and Antonio Porchia are forthcoming from Copper Canyon Press in 2003.

OBAKA THE PILGRIM: See Sam Hamill.

WILLIAM O'DALY is the translator of six volumes of the poetry of Pablo Neruda and author of *The Whale in the Web.* His daughter, Kyra, was born in 1997.

GREGORY ORR is the author of *Orpheus & Eurydice* and *The Caged Owl: New and Selected Poems.* His daughters are Liza and Sophie.

MIKLÓS RADNÓTI was born in Hungary in 1909. His mother and twin brother died during the birth. Several of his greatest poems were written in the labor camps and copper mines of Yugoslavia, where he was forced to work by the Nazis, who later executed him during a forced march. His poems appear in Stephen Berg's *Steel Cricket: Versions 1958–1997.* "Unnoticed" was written November 15, 1943.

KENNETH REXROTH had two daughters, Mary and Katharine. His oeuvre, which includes poetry, translations, and essays, profoundly changed twentieth-century American literature. His poem comes from *The Complete Poems of Kenneth Rexroth.*

ALBERTO RÍOS is the author of *The Smallest Muscle in the Human Body,* among many other books. Born and raised in the American-Mexican border town of Nogales, he now lives in Chandler, Arizona, with his wife, Lupita, and their son, Joaquin.

PRIMUS ST. JOHN was born in New York City and raised by his West Indian grandparents. He is the author of *Communion: Poems 1976–1998,* and he teaches at Portland State University. His daughters are Joy and May.

REBECCA SEIFERLE is the editor of the on-line literary journal *Drunken Boat.* A poet and translator whose most recent collection of poetry is *Bitters,* she is the mother of two daughters, Ann and Maria, and a son, Jacob.

ANN STANFORD was born in 1916 and spent her entire life in California, documenting in her poems its physical and social landscapes as they changed during the twentieth century. Her selected poems are gathered in *Holding Our Own.* She died in 1987.

RUTH STONE was born in Virginia in 1915. She is the author of eight books of poetry and is the recipient of many awards and honors, including the National Book Critics Circle Award and the Cerf Lifetime Achievement Award from the state of Vermont. Her most recent book is *In the Next Galaxy*. She presently lives in Vermont.

JOSEPH STROUD is the author of three books of poetry, including *Below Cold Mountain*. He lives part of the year in Santa Cruz on the California coast, part of the year in a cabin at Shay Creek on the east side of the Sierra Nevada.

KAREN SWENSON can probably lay claim to being America's most widely traveled poet. Besides reading and teaching throughout the United States, she has traveled around the world, frequently venturing throughout Asia, reporting on jailed writers for *The Wall Street Journal* and acting as an unofficial emissary for PEN. Her most recent book is *A Daughter's Latitude: New & Selected Poems*.

ANNA SWIR, a member of the Polish Resistance during the Nazi occupation, served as a military nurse in a makeshift hospital during the Warsaw Uprising. In her poems she rejects the grand gestures that lead to war, in favor of a world cast in miniature. Her poems in *Talking to My Body* were translated by Czesław Miłosz and Leonard Nathan.

ARTHUR SZE is the author of *The Redshifting Web: Poems 1970–1998* and *The Silk Dragon: Translations from the Chinese*. He is the father of Micah and Sarah and lives with his wife, the poet Carol Moldaw, in Pojoaque, New Mexico.

T'AO CH'IEN (365–427 A.D.), equally well known by his given name, T'ao Yüan-ming, stands at the head of the great Chinese poetic tradition like a revered grandfather: profoundly wise, self-possessed, quiet, comforting. T'ao was the first writer to make a poetry of his natural voice and immediate experience, thereby creating the personal lyricism that all major Chinese poets inherited and made their own. The outlines of T'ao Ch'ien's life—his struggle to free himself from the constraints of official life and his eventual commitment to the life of a recluse-farmer, despite poverty and hardship—became one of the central, organizing myths in the Chinese poetic tradition. His poems, translated by David Hinton, are published in *The Selected Poems of T'ao Ch'ien.*

ELAINE TERRANOVA was born in Philadelphia in 1939, grew up in a working-class neighborhood, and has lived in that city ever since. She has held a variety of jobs, including temp worker and copy editor as well as instructor in English and creative writing at Temple University and reading and writing specialist at Community College of Philadelphia. Her book is *Damages.*

ELEANOR WILNER is the author of four previous books of poetry, including *Reversing the Spell: New & Selected Poems.* She holds a Ph.D. from Johns Hopkins University and serves as a contributing editor to *Calyx.* Her awards include a MacArthur Fellowship, the Juniper Prize, and a Pushcart Prize. She teaches at Warren Wilson College and lives in Philadelphia.

C.D. WRIGHT teaches at Brown University and in 1994 was named State Poet of Rhode Island. She is the author of nine books of poetry, including *Deepstep Come Shining* and *Steal Away: Selected and New Poems.* With her husband, Forrest Gander, she edits Lost Roads Publishers. Their son is Brecht.

GAIL WRONSKY received a B.A. and an M.F.A. from the University of Virginia and a Ph.D. from the University of Utah. She is the author of two books of poetry, including *Dying for Beauty*, and teaches at Loyola-Marymount University in Los Angeles, where she lives with her husband, Chuck Rosenthal, and their daughter, Marlena.

About the Editor

MICHAEL WIEGERS is the editor of *This Art: Poems about Poetry* and co-editor (with Mónica de la Torre) of *Reversible Monuments: Contemporary Mexican Poetry*. He is Managing Editor of Copper Canyon Press and lives in Port Townsend with Katherine Garfield and their brilliant, beautiful daughter, Ella.

Copper Canyon Press gratefully acknowledges the support of
TARGET STORES
for their assistance in publishing this book.

The Chinese character for poetry is made up of two parts: "word" and "temple." It also serves as pressmark for Copper Canyon Press.

Founded in 1972, Copper Canyon Press remains dedicated to publishing poetry exclusively, from Nobel laureates to new and emerging authors. The Press thrives with the generous patronage of readers, writers, booksellers, librarians, teachers, students, and funders—everyone who shares the conviction that poetry invigorates the language and sharpens our appreciation of the world.

PUBLISHERS' CIRCLE
The Allen Foundation for the Arts
Lannan Foundation
Lila Wallace—Reader's Digest Fund
National Endowment for the Arts

EDITORS' CIRCLE
Thatcher Bailey
The Breneman Jaech Foundation
Cynthia Hartwig and Tom Booster
Port Townsend Paper Company
Target Stores
Emily Warn and Daj Oberg
Washington State Arts Commission

FOR INFORMATION AND CATALOGS:
COPPER CANYON PRESS
Post Office Box 271
Port Townsend, Washington 98368
877/501-1393
www.coppercanyonpress.org

The interior of this book was designed and typeset by Phil Kovacevich using Quark Xpress 4.1 on a Macintosh G4. The typeface, Requiem, is derived from a set of inscriptional capitals appearing in Ludovico degli Arrighi's 1523 writing manual, *Il modo de temperare le penne*. This book was printed by Malloy, Inc.